English to a Beat!

Jane Zion Brauer

Practice Book

HAMPTON-BROWN

T0050794

Contents

Skills Practice

Skill Plan 1 Verbs: *Am, Is, Are* 4–6
Skill Plan 2 Subject Pronouns 7–9
Skill Plan 3 Questions with *Yes/No* and Short Answers 10–12
Skill Plan 4 Sentence Types 13–15
Skill Plan 5 Verbs: Present Progressive Form 16–18
Skill Plan 6 Nouns: Singular and Plural 19–21
Skill Plan 7 Adjectives 22–24
Skill Plan 8 Subjects and Verbs 25–27
Skill Plan 9 Possessives: Nouns and Pronouns 28–30
Skill Plan 10 Verb Tense: Present and Past 31–33
Skill Plan 11 Prepositions 34–36
Skill Plan 12 Irregular Verbs: Past Tense 37–39
Skill Plan 13 Verbs: Future Tense; Modals 40–42
Skill Plan 14 Object Pronouns 43–45
Skill Plan 15 Questions with Elaborated Answers 46–48
Skill Plan 16 Adjectives: Comparatives and Superlatives 49–51

Writing Projects

Skill Plan 1 Fan Mail 55–56
Skill Plan 2 Picture Album 57–58
Skill Plan 3 Interview 59–60
Skill Plan 4 Cartoon Strip 61–62
Skill Plan 5 Survey Results 63–64
Skill Plan 6 Graph 65–66
Skill Plan 7 Descriptive Sentences 67–68
Skill Plan 8 Sequence Paragraph 69–70
Skill Plan 9 Comparison Paragraph 71–72
Skill Plan 10 Story 73–74
Skill Plan 11 Description of a Place 75–76
Skill Plan 12 Personal Narrative 77–78
Skill Plan 13 Advice Column 79–80
Skill Plan 14 Journal Entry 81–82
Skill Plan 15 Script 83–84
Skill Plan 16 Book Review 85–86

Skill Tests

Skill Test 1 88
Skill Test 2 89
Skill Test 3 90
Skill Test 4 91
Skill Test 5 92
Skill Test 6 93
Skill Test 7 94
Skill Test 8 95
Skill Test 9 96
Skill Test 10 97
Skill Test 11 98
Skill Test 12 99
Skill Test 13 100
Skill Test 14 101
Skill Test 15 102
Skill Test 16 103

Name _____ Date _____

Statements with *I am*

Look at the picture.

Choose a word or words from the box to complete each sentence.
Write the word or words.

I am I'm

1. I ___am___ Boris.
2. _____ am 13 years old.
3. I _____ from Russia.
4. _____ a good artist.
5. _____ happy.
6. _____ funny.

Write four sentences about yourself.
Use *I am* and *I'm*.
Then draw a picture of yourself.

7. _____

_____

8. _____

_____

9. _____

_____

10. _____

_____

© Hampton-Brown

Name _____ Date _____

Statements with *You are*

Read the sentences.

Choose a word from the box to complete each sentence. Write the word.

You are You're

1. I am big. You ___are___ little.

2. _____ are so pretty.

3. _____ are a good tailor.

4. _____ a fast worker!

5. Now you _____ big!

6. _____ little again.

© Hampton-Brown

Name _____ Date _____

Statements with *Is* and *Are*

Read the sentences. Look at the picture.

Write *is* or *are* to complete each sentence.

1. The dress ___is___ not right.
2. The dress _____ too big.
3. The gloves _____ not right.
4. The gloves _____ too small.
5. The shoes _____ too big.
6. The shoes _____ too loose.
7. The hat _____ the right size.
8. The hat _____ perfect!

Write a sentence about each picture. Use *is* or *are*.

9. The socks _____

10. The jacket _____

11. The boots _____

12. The skirt _____

© Hampton-Brown

Name _____ Date _____

Pronouns: *I, You, We*

Look at the pictures.

Write *I*, *You*, or *We* to complete each sentence.

1.

2.

3.

4.

5.

6.

© Hampton-Brown

Name _____ Date _____

Pronouns: *He, She*

Look at the pictures. Read the sentences.

Change the underlined word to a pronoun. Write *He* or *She*.

1. Mom digs in the garden.

She digs in the garden.

2. Grandma has a big hat.

_____ has a big hat.

3. Dad picks the peppers.

_____ picks the peppers.

4. Ahn sprays the water.

_____ sprays the water.

5. Tran runs away!

_____ runs away!

6. Dad smiles.

_____ smiles.

© Hampton-Brown

Name _____ Date _____

Pronouns: *It*, *They*

Look at each picture. Read the sentences.

Change the underlined words to a pronoun.
Write *It* or *They*.

1. Boris and Lena get carrots.

   They get carrots.

2. The carrots are big.

   _____ are big.

3. The carrot is good.

   _____ is good.

4. Nura and Hadi get tomatoes.

   _____ get tomatoes.

5. The tomatoes are beautiful.

   _____ are beautiful.

6. The bag is full!

   _____ is full!

© Hampton-Brown

Name _____ Date _____

Questions with *Can*

Look at the picture.

Choose words from the box to complete each question and answer. Write the words.

Can	can	can't
Yes	No	

Questions

1. Can the boy catch the ball?
2. _____ the girl kick the ball?
3. _____ the boy throw the ball?
4. _____ the girl run?
5. _____ the kids jump?
6. _____ the dog play?
7. _____ the boy swing up high?
8. _____ the girl swing up high?

Answers

No, he can't.

_____, she can't.

Yes, he _____.

_____, she can.

Yes, they _____.

No, he _____.

Yes, he _____.

No, she _____.

© Hampton-Brown

Name _____ Date _____

Questions with *Is* and *Are*

Look at pages 20–21 in *Can Turtle Fly*?

Choose words from the box to complete each question and answer. Write the words.

Is	is	isn't
Are	are	aren't

Questions

1. Are the birds in the sky?
2. _____ Turtle in the sky?
3. _____ Turtle sad?
4. _____ the clouds dark and gray?
5. _____ the stick in Turtle's mouth?
6. _____ the trees and mountains small?
7. _____ Turtle happy?
8. _____ the trees in the sky?

Answers

Yes, they are.
Yes, he _____.
No, he _____.
No, they _____.
Yes, it _____.
Yes, they _____.
Yes, he _____.
No, they _____.

Now look at pages 22–23 in *Can Turtle Fly*?

Write questions about the picture.

Find a partner. Ask your questions.

9. Is _____
10. Is _____
11. Are _____
12. Are _____

© Hampton-Brown

Name _____ Date _____

Who? What? When? Where?

In the Question	In the Answer
Who	a person
What	a thing
When	a time
Where	a place

Look at each picture. Read the question.

Write the answer.

1.

Where is the kite?

The kite is in the air.

2.

When is lunch?

_____

3.

Who is on the swing?

_____

4.

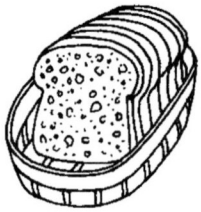

What is in the basket?

_____

Write four more questions.

Have a partner answer the questions.

5. Who _____

6. What _____

7. When _____

8. Where _____

© Hampton-Brown

Name _____ Date _____

Commands

Look at the map. Follow the numbers.

Write a command for each number. Tell Janell what to do.

Commands
Walk to the _____.
Go to the _____.
Stay on the _____.
Leave the _____.

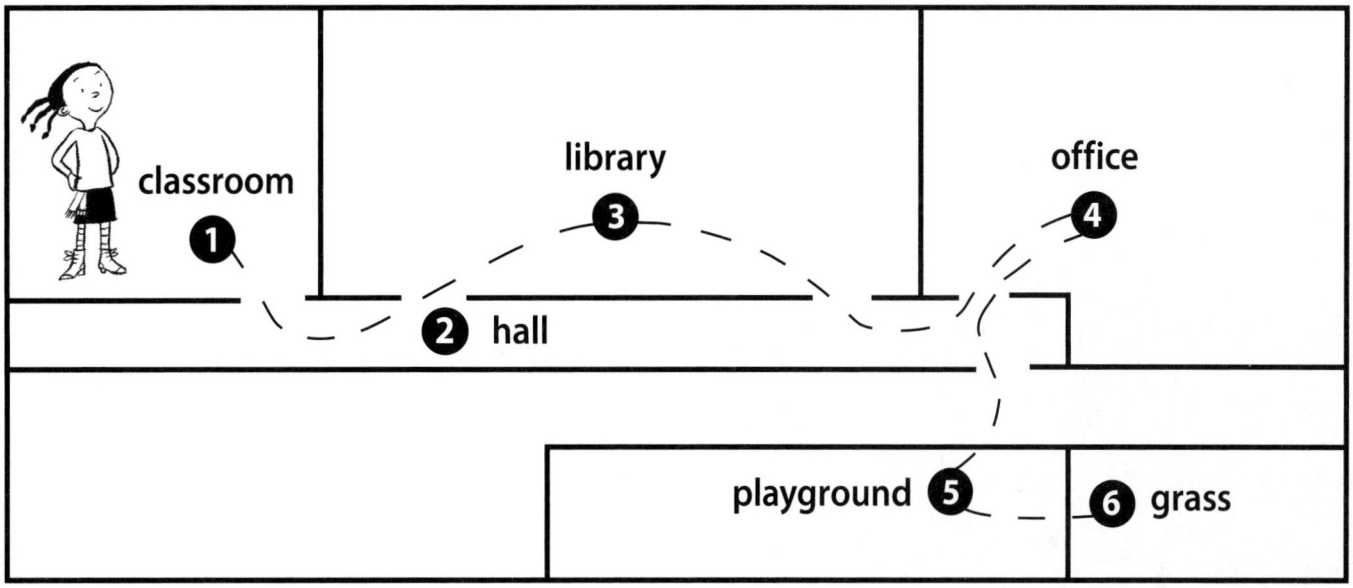

1. Leave the classroom.

2. _____

3. _____

4. _____

5. _____

6. _____

© Hampton-Brown

Name _____ Date _____

Questions and Exclamations

Read each sentence.

Write a question mark (?) or an exclamation point (!).

1. Is the fire gone ?_____
2. The fire is gone _____
3. Is the elephant happy _____
4. The elephant is angry _____
5. Are the bees in the elephant's nose _____
6. Will the bees leave _____
7. The elephant blows and blows _____
8. Can the bees find a new home _____
9. Where will the bees go _____
10. The elephant's nose is very long _____

Look at pages 28–29 in *Leave, Bees!*

Write two questions and two exclamations about the pictures.

11. **Question:** _____
12. **Question:** _____
13. **Exclamation:** _____
14. **Exclamation:** _____

© Hampton-Brown

Name _____ Date _____

Statements with *Not*

Look at the picture. Read each question.

Write the answer. Use *not*.

1. Is the door open? *No, the door is not open.*

2. Is the police officer inside? _____

3. Are the boys in the car? _____

4. Are the boys scared? _____

5. Is the librarian angry? _____

6. Is the police officer worried? _____

7. Are the boys at home? _____

8. Is the librarian in the car? _____

9. Are the boys on the steps? _____

10. Is it a rainy day? _____

© Hampton-Brown

Name _____ Date _____

Action Verbs with *-ing*

Look at each picture.

Choose a word from the box to complete each sentence. Add *-ing*. Write the new word.

walk	eat	talk
play	smell	sing

1.

They are eating breakfast.

2.

She is _____ to school.

3.

She is _____ a song.

4.

She is _____ the soup.

5.

They are _____ to Dad.

6.

They are _____ a game.

© Hampton-Brown

Name _____ Date _____

Action Verbs with *-ing*

Look at the picture.

Use each group of words to write a question. Add a question mark.

1. is | the woman | smelling | What — *What is the woman smelling?*

2. Dad | carrying | Is | a basket — _____

3. holding | is | What | Janell — _____

4. Are | crying | the babies — _____

5. Where | standing | the girls | are — _____

6. Janell | water | drinking | Is — _____

© Hampton-Brown

Name _____ Date _____

Action Verbs with *-ing*

Look at each picture. Read the question. Write the rest of the answer.

1.

Are you eating a mango?

No, I *am not eating a mango.*

2.

Are you eating a plum?

Yes, I _____

3.

Is the cat drinking milk?

No, it _____

4.

Are the cats drinking water?

Yes, they _____

© Hampton-Brown

Name _____ Date _____

Nouns

cook	town	farm
horse	king	pot
tree	chick	

Look at each picture.

Write a word from the box to name the picture.
Tell if it is a **person**, **animal**, **place**, or **thing**.

1.

chick

animal

2.

_____

_____

3.

_____

_____

4.

_____

_____

5.

_____

_____

6.

_____

_____

7.

_____

_____

8.

_____

_____

© Hampton-Brown

Name _____ Date _____

Plural Nouns with -s

Look at the picture. Read each sentence.

Change the word below the blank to tell about more than one.
Write the new word.

1. The little chicks are in the barnyard.
   chick

2. There are two _____ in the barnyard, too.
   pig

3. The _____ sit on the fence. They watch the pigs.
   girl

4. The _____ have a lot of apples on them.
   tree

5. The hungry _____ eat the sweet apples.
   horse

6. The _____ are hungry, too! They run to the barn.
   goat

7. There are two _____ standing in the barn.
   farmer

8. The _____ fly over the barn.
   bird

© Hampton-Brown

Name _____ Date _____

Irregular Plural Nouns

Look at the picture. Read each sentence.

Change each sentence to tell about more than one.
Use a word from the box. Write the new sentence.

children	mice
women	feet
geese	men

1. The child is swimming.

The children are swimming.

2. The goose is flying.

_____

3. The woman is eating.

_____

4. Her foot is in the water.

_____

5. The mouse is running.

_____

6. The man is working.

_____

© Hampton-Brown

Name _____ Date _____

Adjectives That Tell How Many

1 one	**6** six
2 two	**7** seven
3 three	**8** eight
4 four	**9** nine
5 five	**10** ten

Look at the pictures. Read what Simon says.

Write number words to tell how many more of each item Simon needs.

Ten people are coming to my party!

1. Simon has **three**  . He needs seven forks.

2. Simon has **six**  . He needs _____ plates.

3. Simon has **two**  . He needs _____ chairs.

4. Simon has **seven**  . He needs _____ cups.

5. Simon has **five**  . He needs _____ spoons.

6. Simon has **eight**  . He needs _____ napkins.

Look at the pictures.

Write two sentences about the things for Simon's party. Use number words.

7. _____

8. _____

© Hampton-Brown

Name _____ Date _____

Adjectives That Describe

blue	red	long
brown	big	round
green	little	square

Color the picture.

Complete each sentence. Use two different words from the box. Write the words.

1.

It's a brown box.

The box is square.

2.

It's a _____ bag.

The bag is _____.

3.

It's a _____ scarf.

The scarf is _____.

4.

It's a _____ car.

The car is _____.

5.

It's a _____ ball.

The ball is _____.

6.

It's a _____ hat.

The hat is _____.

© Hampton-Brown

Name _____ Date _____

This, That, These, Those

this	these
that	those

Read each person's sentence. Find the food in the picture.

Write a word from the box to complete the sentence.

1. This soup smells good!
2. _____ cake over there is pretty.
3. Please pass _____ cookies to me.
4. _____ noodles are really hot!
5. Would you like _____ green beans?
6. _____ ham looks so yummy!
7. Will you pass _____ potatoes to me?
8. May I have _____ salt, please?

© Hampton-Brown

Name _____ Date _____

Subjects and Action Verbs

run	climb
sit	jump
race	drink

Look at the pictures.

Choose a word from the box to complete each sentence.
Write the word.

Write two more sentences. Use action verbs.
Start your sentences with *I*, *You*, *We*, or *They*.

5. _____

6. _____

© Hampton-Brown

Name _____ Date _____

Action Verbs with -s

Read the sentences.

Choose the correct verb.
Write it in the blank.

1. I ___throw___ the ball into the air.
   throw / throws

2. Janell _____ toward the ball.
   run / runs

3. Janell is too slow! The ball _____ to the ground.
   fall / falls

4. The people watch. They _____ loudly.
   yell / yells

5. José _____ the ball. It _____ from his hands!
   grab / grabs slip / slips

6. Janell _____ the ball. She _____ to the line.
   get / gets race / races

7. We _____ the game! The people _____.
   win / wins cheer / cheers

Write three more sentences about a game. Use action verbs.

8. She _____

9. He _____

10. It _____

© Hampton-Brown

Name _____ Date _____

Verbs: *Have* and *Has*

Complete each sentence. Write *have* or *has*.

1. The Sky God ___has___ a gift for Anansi.

2. Now Anansi _____ all the wisdom in the world!

3. He climbs a tree. It _____ a tall trunk.

4. The animals _____ a question. They ask why Anansi falls.

5. Anansi's son _____ an idea.

6. Anansi's son _____ more wisdom than Anansi.

7. Anansi breaks the pot! Now, I _____ wisdom.

8. You _____ wisdom, too!

Write two more sentences about Anansi or another character. Use *have* or *has*.

Read your sentences to a partner.

9. _____

10. _____

© Hampton-Brown

Name _____ Date _____

Nouns with 's

Look at the pictures.

Write the correct noun to complete each sentence. Add 's.

1. This is the cook's spoon.

2. This is the _____ basket.

3. This is the _____ cup.

4. These are the _____ rolls.

5. This is _____ brush.

6. This is the _____ bowl.

7. This is the _____ hat.

8. This is the _____ tray.

© Hampton-Brown

Name _____ Date _____

Pronouns: *My, Your, Our*

Look at the pictures.

Choose the correct pronoun to complete each sentence. Write the word.

1. Welcome to The Clothes Line! This is ___my___ store.
my / I

2. You have nice clothes in _____ store.
your / my

3. This is _____ favorite place to shop.
our / we

4. We always buy _____ clothes here.
I / our

5. This is not my hat. Is it _____ hat?
your / you

6. Yes, it is _____ hat. Thank you!
our / my

© Hampton-Brown

Name _____ Date _____

Pronouns: *His, Her, Its, Their*

Look at pages 20–27 in *María and the Baker's Bread.*

Complete each sentence. Write a pronoun from the box. Be sure it goes with the underlined part of the sentence.

his	her
its	their

1. At the court, the baker tells ___his___ story.
2. Then, María tells _____ story.
3. María talks about the bread. She loves _____ smell.
4. The judge will think about _____ answer.
5. The courthouse closes. People wait outside _____ doors.
6. Finally, the judge gives _____ answer to María and the baker.
7. He wants María to put three coins in _____ cup.
8. The friends help María. They put _____ coins in the cup.
9. The judge shakes the coins. Everyone hears _____ sound.
10. The judge tells María to keep _____ coins.
11. She celebrates with _____ friends.
12. The baker is mad! He shakes _____ fists.

© Hampton-Brown

Name _____ Date _____

Verb Tense

Look at the picture. Read each sentence.

Change the verb to tell about the past. Write the new sentence.

1. The ants crawl over the log.

The ants crawled over the log.

2. The frog kicks his legs.

_____

3. The spider walks on the leaf.

_____

4. The leaf covers some sticks.

_____

5. The grasshopper jumps over the rocks.

_____

6. The birds land on the grass.

_____

© Hampton-Brown

Name _____ Date _____

Actions in the Past: *-ed*

Look at the picture.

Change the word in front of each sentence to tell about the past.
Write the new word.

show	**1.** Simon *showed* his mouse to the class.
smile	**2.** Janell _____ at the nice mouse.
like	**3.** Janell _____ its cute little nose.
close	**4.** Nura _____ her eyes.
hate	**5.** She _____ the scary mouse!
walk	**6.** José _____ to the cage.
play	**7.** He _____ with the mouse.
touch	**8.** His hand _____ the soft fur.
smell	**9.** The mouse _____ his fingers.
decide	**10.** José _____ to get a mouse, too!

© Hampton-Brown

Name _____ Date _____

Actions in the Past: *-ed*

Look at each picture.

Change the word under the blank to tell about the past. Write the word.

1.

The frog slipped off the log.
slip

2.

She _____ into the water.
drop

3.

She _____ up and down.
bob

4.

She _____ across the water.
splash

5.

She _____ onto a lily pad.
hop

6.

She _____ a fly.
watch

7.

She _____ out of the pond.
jump

8.

She _____ on a leaf.
stop

© Hampton-Brown

Name _____ Date _____

Location Words: *In, On*

Look at pages 12–13 in *Juan Bobo Goes Up and Down the Hill.*

Write *in* or *on* to complete each sentence.

1. Grandma is ___in___ the house.
2. The hat is _____ Juan's hand.
3. The cupboard is _____ the floor.
4. The shelf is _____ the cupboard.
5. The dishes are _____ the shelf.
6. The black pot is _____ the cupboard.
7. The bowl is _____ the shelf.
8. The coconuts are _____ the bowl.

Now look at page 14 in *Juan Bobo Goes Up and Down the Hill.*

Write three sentences about the picture. Use *in* and *on*.

9. _____
10. _____
11. _____

Read the sentences.

Draw a picture about them in the box.

12. The table is in the kitchen. The bowl is on the table. Some fruit is in the bowl.

© Hampton-Brown

Name _____ Date _____

More Location Words

below	inside	in front of
behind	above	beside
next to	under	

Look at the pictures.

Choose a word or words from the box to complete each sentence. Write the word.

1. José is in front of the closet.
2. The shirts are _____ the closet.
3. The shoes are _____ the shirts.
4. The hats are _____ the shirts.
5. The desk is _____ the closet.
6. The window is _____ the chair.
7. The chair is _____ the desk.
8. The dog is _____ the chair.

© Hampton-Brown

Name _____ Date _____

Direction Words

down	up
across	into
through	

Look at the picture. Follow the arrows.

Choose a word from the box to complete each sentence. Write the word.

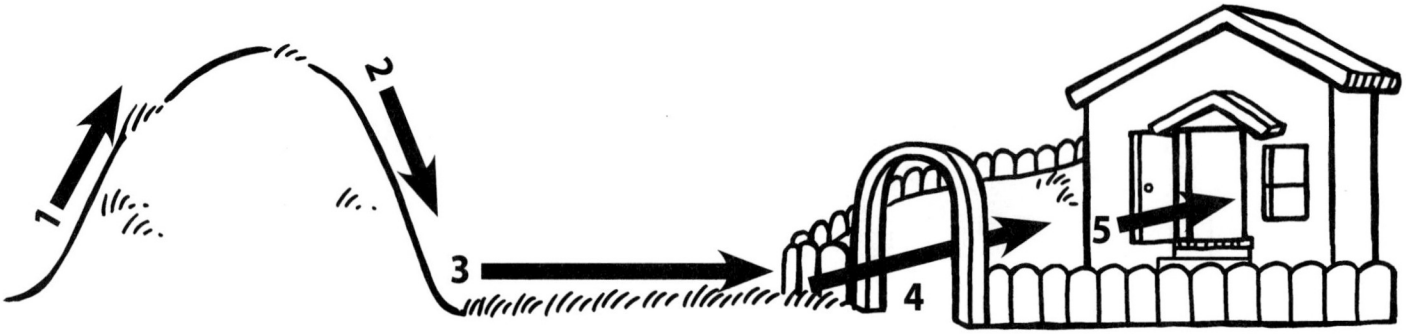

Go ___up___ the hill. Walk _____ the hill.
1. **2.**

Go _____ the grass. Walk _____ the gate.
3. **4.**

Go _____ the house.
5.

Look at the picture. Follow the arrows.

Write three sentences. Tell where to go. Use words from the box.

6. _____

_____

7. _____

_____

8. _____

_____

© Hampton-Brown

Name _____ Date _____

Verbs: *Was* and *Were*

Look at pages 8–9 in *The Brother Who Gave Rice.*

Complete each sentence. Write *was* or *were.*

1. The children ___were___ at the table.
2. They _____ happy.
3. The baby _____ on the floor.
4. He _____ asleep.
5. The dishes _____ on the table.
6. The baskets _____ on the shelf.
7. The rice _____ hot.
8. The food _____ good.
9. It _____ a nice dinner.
10. The father said, "I _____ hungry. Now I'm full!"
11. The mother said, "We _____ all hungry!"

Now look at page 32 in *The Brother Who Gave Rice.*

Write five sentences about the picture. Use *was* or *were.*

12. _____
13. _____
14. _____
15. _____
16. _____

© Hampton-Brown

Name _____ Date _____

Irregular Verbs

Look at the picture. Read the sentences.

Change each sentence to tell about the past.
Use a verb from the box. Write the new sentence.

had	took
sat	gave
got	found
went	brought

Now	In the Past
1. Our family goes to the park.	Our family went to the park.
2. Mom brings a lot of food!	_____
3. We find a good table.	_____
4. We sit at the table.	_____
5. Dad takes out the food.	_____
6. I get the plates.	_____
7. I give rice to my brother.	_____
8. We all have a great time.	_____

© Hampton-Brown

Name _____ Date _____

More Irregular Verbs

saw	felt
left	said
made	came

Look at the pictures.

Choose a word from the box to complete each sentence. Write the word.

1.

Yesterday, Yong and I ___came___ home from school.

2.

We _____ hungry.

3.

We _____ sandwiches.

4.

Then we _____ with our food.

5.

Mom _____ the mess.

6.

She _____, "Clean this up!"

© Hampton-Brown

Name _____ Date _____

Actions in the Future

will	is going to
Will	am going to
won't	are going to

Look at the picture.

Choose a word or words from the box to complete each sentence. Write the word or words.

1. "We *are going to* hike to the lake!" said the ranger.
2. "_____ you hike with us?" Ruth asked Monika.
3. "Yes, I _____ hike with you," Monika said.
4. "I hope the hike _____ be long," Monika added. "I'm tired."
5. "Be careful! That bee _____ sting you," said the ranger.
6. "The sun is hot. I _____ wear my hat now," said Ruth.
7. "When _____ we eat lunch?" asked Monika.
8. "We _____ eat at 12:00," the ranger said.

© Hampton-Brown

Name _____ Date _____

Can, Could, and Would

Look at each picture.

Complete the sentences. Write *can*, *could*, or *would*.

© Hampton-Brown

Name _____ Date _____

Must and *Should*

Look at the picture. Read the sign.

Write three sentences. Tell what Lorena *must* do when she hikes.

1. _____

_____

2. _____

_____

3. _____

_____

Look at the picture.

Write three sentences.
Tell what Lorena *should* do when she hikes.

4. _____

_____

5. _____

_____

6. _____

_____

© Hampton-Brown

Name _____ Date _____

Pronouns: *Me, You, Us*

Look at each picture.

Write *me, you,* or *us* to complete the sentence.

1.

I want to make a card for Dad.
Will you help ___me___ ?

2.

Yes! We can work together. Then the card will be from _____ .

3.

How can I help _____ ?

4.

Please give _____ the scissors.

5.

I'll give _____ the markers, too.

6.

Dad will love this card from _____ !

© Hampton-Brown

Name _____ Date _____

Pronouns: *Him, Her*

Read each sentence.

Change the underlined word to *him* or *her*. Write the new sentence.

1. Yesterday, the kids had a party for Mom.

Yesterday, the kids had a party for her.

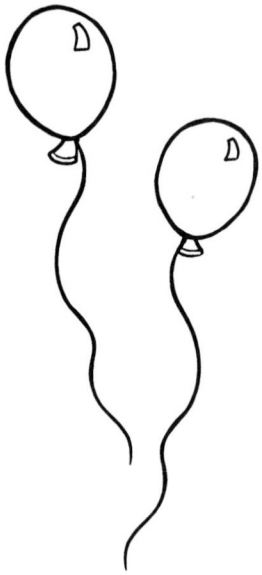

2. They made Mom a gift.

_____

3. Ivan asked Marie to get the gift.

_____

4. Marie handed the gift to Ivan.

_____

5. Ivan gave the gift to Mom.

_____

6. Mom smiled and hugged Ivan.

_____

7. Mom hugged Marie, too.

_____

8. Then Mom showed Dad the gift.

_____

© Hampton-Brown

Name _____ Date _____

Pronouns: *It, Them*

Look at pages 18–21 in *Bring Me Three Gifts!*

Read each sentence. Change the underlined words to *it* or *them*. Write the new sentence.

1. The wives had <u>three gifts</u>.

The wives had them.

2. The first wife held <u>the lantern</u>.

_____

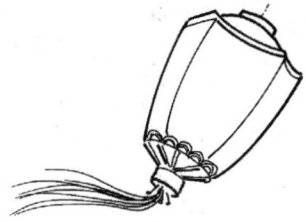

3. The second wife waved <u>the fan</u>.

_____

4. The third wife carried <u>the chimes</u>.

_____

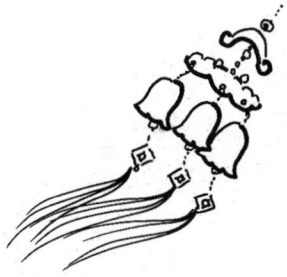

5. Father liked <u>the gifts</u>.

_____

6. He smiled at <u>the three wives</u>.

_____

Now look at pages 24–25 in *Bring Me Three Gifts!*

Write two sentences about the picture. Use *it* and *them*.

Read your sentences to a partner. Point to the things in the picture to show *it* or *them*.

7. _____

8. _____

© Hampton-Brown

Name _____ Date _____

Questions with *Do* and *Does*

Look at the picture. Think of questions to ask each girl.

Write your questions.

Trade papers with a partner.

Answer your partner's questions.

1. **Question:** Do you like to sleep outside?

   Answer: Yes, I do!

2. **Question:** Does

   Answer: _____

3. **Question:** Do

   Answer: _____

4. **Question:** Does

   Answer: _____

5. **Question:** Do

   Answer: _____

6. **Question:** Does

   Answer: _____

© Hampton-Brown

Name _____ Date _____

Questions with *Why*

Draw a line to the words that finish each question.

1. Why is Hodja sleep outside?

2. Why does Kemal so unhappy?

3. Why do Hodja's eyes closed?

4. Why are Kemal and Hodja go to Kemal's house?

Look at *Does a Candle Keep You Warm?*

Write four more questions about the story or the characters.

Trade papers with a partner. Answer your partner's questions.

5. Question: Why _____

Answer: _____

6. Question: Why _____

Answer: _____

7. Question: Why _____

Answer: _____

8. Question: Why _____

Answer: _____

© Hampton-Brown

Name _____ Date _____

Questions with *How*

Look at the picture.

Write questions about the picture.
Use *How, How much,* or *How many.*

Trade papers with a partner.

Answer your partner's questions.

1. Question: How strong is the wind?

Answer: It is very strong!

2. Question: _____

Answer: _____

3. Question: _____

Answer: _____

4. Question: _____

Answer: _____

5. Question: _____

Answer: _____

6. Question: _____

Answer: _____

© Hampton-Brown

Name _____ Date _____

Adjectives with *-er* and *-est*

Choose the correct form of the adjective to complete each sentence. Write the word.

1. Today is the ___darkest___ day of the week.
dark / darkest

2. The clouds are _____ today than yesterday.
darker / darkest

3. The raindrops are _____ than the bees!
larger / largest

4. They are the _____ raindrops I've ever seen.
bigest / biggest

5. It is _____ today than Tuesday.
weter / wetter

6. It is the _____ day of the month.
wettest / wet

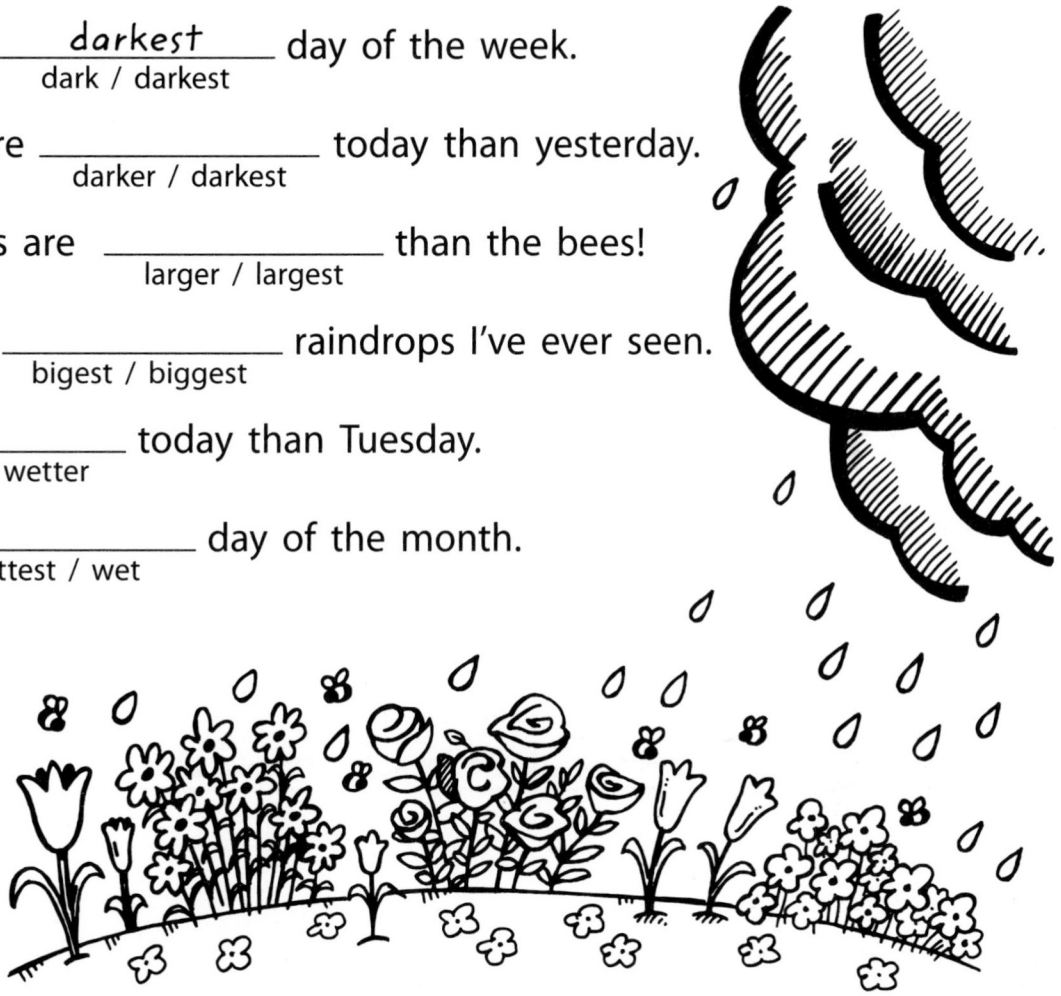

Write four sentences about the weather.
Compare this week's weather to last week's weather.
Use *hotter, hottest, colder,* and *coldest*.

7. _____

8. _____

9. _____

10. _____

© Hampton-Brown

Name _____ Date _____

Adjectives with *More* and *Most*

Complete each sentence. Use *more* or *most* with the word below the blank. Write the words.

1. Daughter Mouse is more beautiful than the stars.
   beautiful
2. She is the _____ mouse in the world!
   beautiful
3. Field Mouse is _____ than the Sun.
   powerful
4. He is the _____ one of all!
   powerful
5. Daughter Mouse thinks love is _____ than beauty.
   important
6. Love is the _____ thing in the universe.
   important

Draw a picture about something exciting and interesting. Write four sentences about it. Use *more* and *most*.

7. _____
8. _____
9. _____
10. _____

© Hampton-Brown

Name _____ Date _____

Comparisons with *Good* and *Bad*

Look at the picture.

Choose the correct form of the adjective to complete each sentence.
Write the word.

1. The mice have a ___good___ time at the party.
   good / best
2. It is the _____ party all year!
   better / best
3. The cake is delicious. It is really _____ .
   worse / good
4. The cake is _____ than the cookies.
   better / gooder
5. Poor Papa Mouse is a _____ dancer!
   worse / bad
6. He is a _____ dancer than Mama Mouse.
   worse / worst
7. Papa Mouse is the _____ dancer in the family.
   worst / baddest
8. He is happy, though. This is the _____ day in his life!
   better / best

© Hampton-Brown

Writing Projects

Writing Help

STEP
1 Prewrite

Plan what you will write.

- Think of ideas.
- Choose an idea.
- Decide who your readers will be.
- Write details about your idea.

STEP
2 Draft

Write fast. Turn your details into sentences. Don't worry about mistakes!

STEP
3 Revise

Make changes. Talk about your draft with a partner. Ask:

✓ Did I use good words?
✓ Is my writing interesting?
✓ Is everything in order?
✓ Did I include enough details?

Revising and Proofreading Marks

Mark	Meaning
^	Add.
⁓	Take out.
⁓^	Change to this.
⁓	Move to here.
^,	Add a comma.
⊙	Add a period.
≡	Capitalize.
⬭	Check spelling.

STEP
4 Edit and Proofread

Look for mistakes. Check spelling and punctuation.

STEP
5 Publish

Make a final copy of your work. Share it with family and friends.

© Hampton-Brown

I'm a Big Fan!

Name:

Dear _____ ,

Address

© Hampton-Brown

© Hampton-Brown

My Picture Album

© Hampton-Brown

© Hampton-Brown

Interview

1. What is your name?

_____

2. Where are you from?

_____

3. When is your birthday?

_____

4. Who is in your family? _____

_____

5. Can you _____

_____

6. Can you _____

_____

7. _____

_____

© Hampton-Brown

© Hampton-Brown

What Happens?

1.

2.

3.

4.

© Hampton-Brown

"The Elephants and the Bees" By _____

1	2
3	4

© Hampton-Brown

Survey

Time: _____ in the ❑ morning ❑ evening ❑ afternoon ❑ night

What are you doing?

Activity	Number of People

© Hampton-Brown

What Is Everyone Doing?

Time: _____ in the ❑ morning ❑ evening ❑ afternoon ❑ night

_____

_____

_____

_____

_____

_____

_____

_____

_____

_____

_____

_____

_____

_____

_____

_____

© Hampton-Brown

Do You Have Pets?

1. What pets do you have?
2. How many do you have?

Name	Pets

© Hampton-Brown

Pets in My School

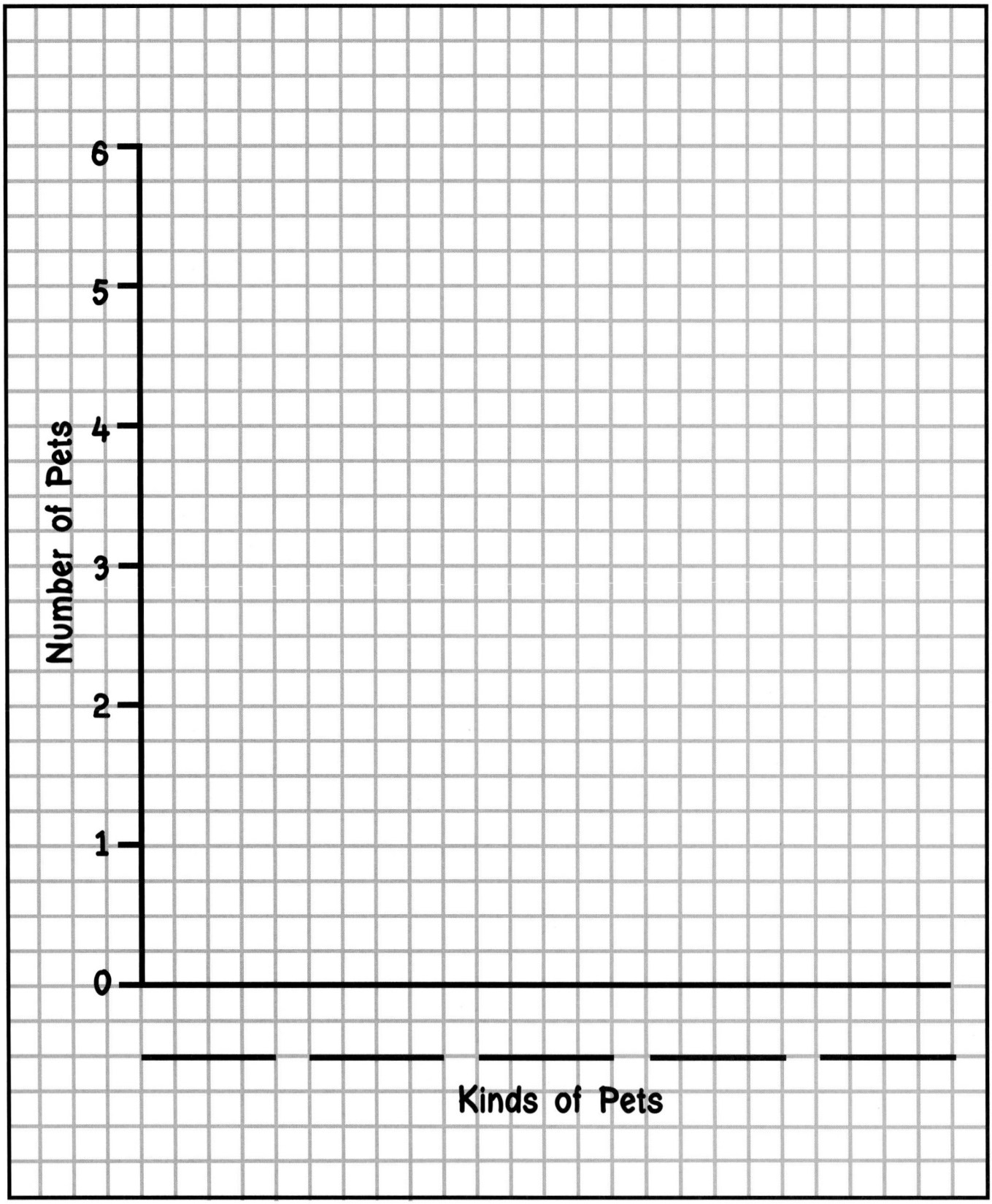

© Hampton-Brown

My Best Gift

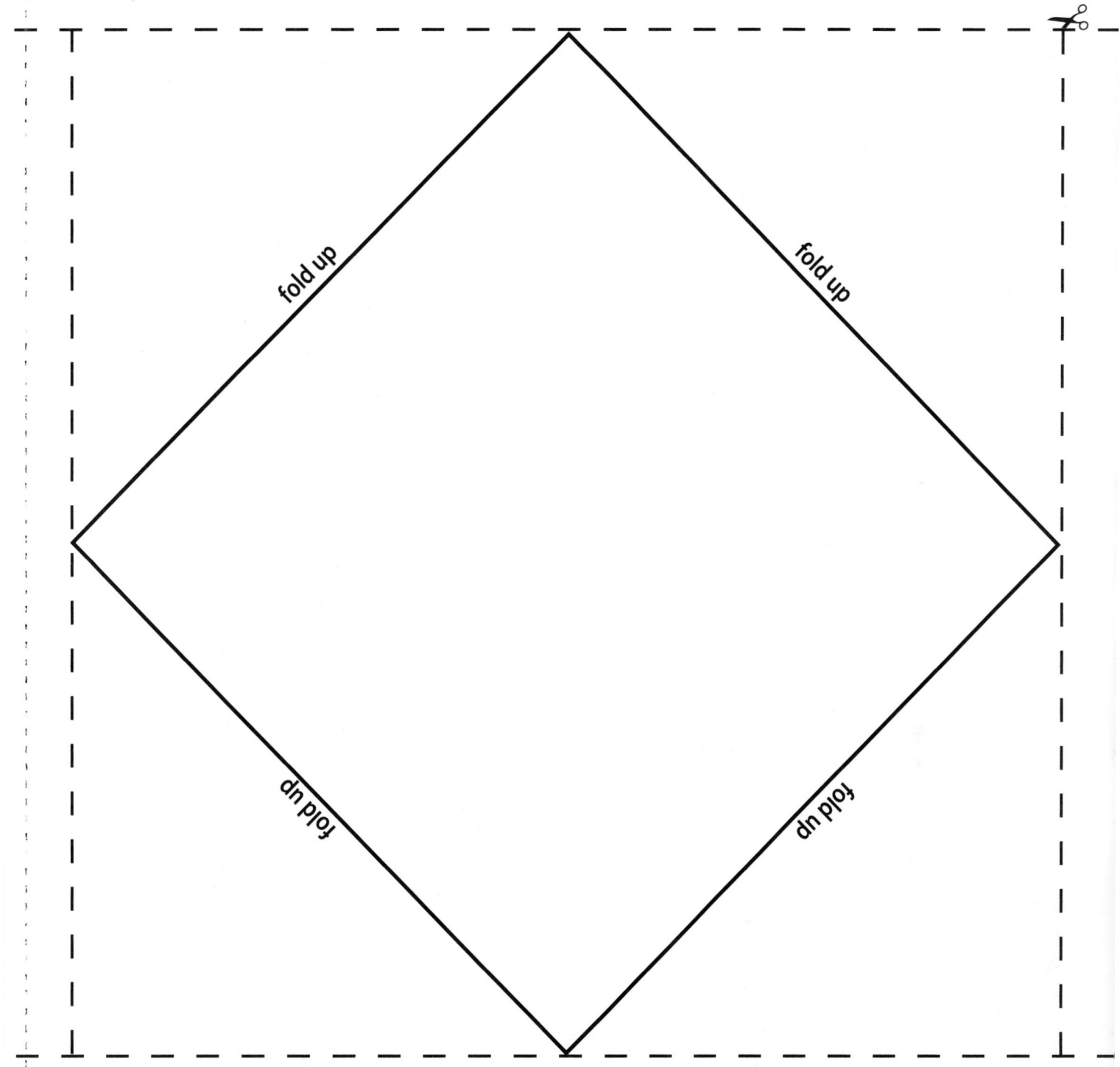

© Hampton-Brown

All About My Gift

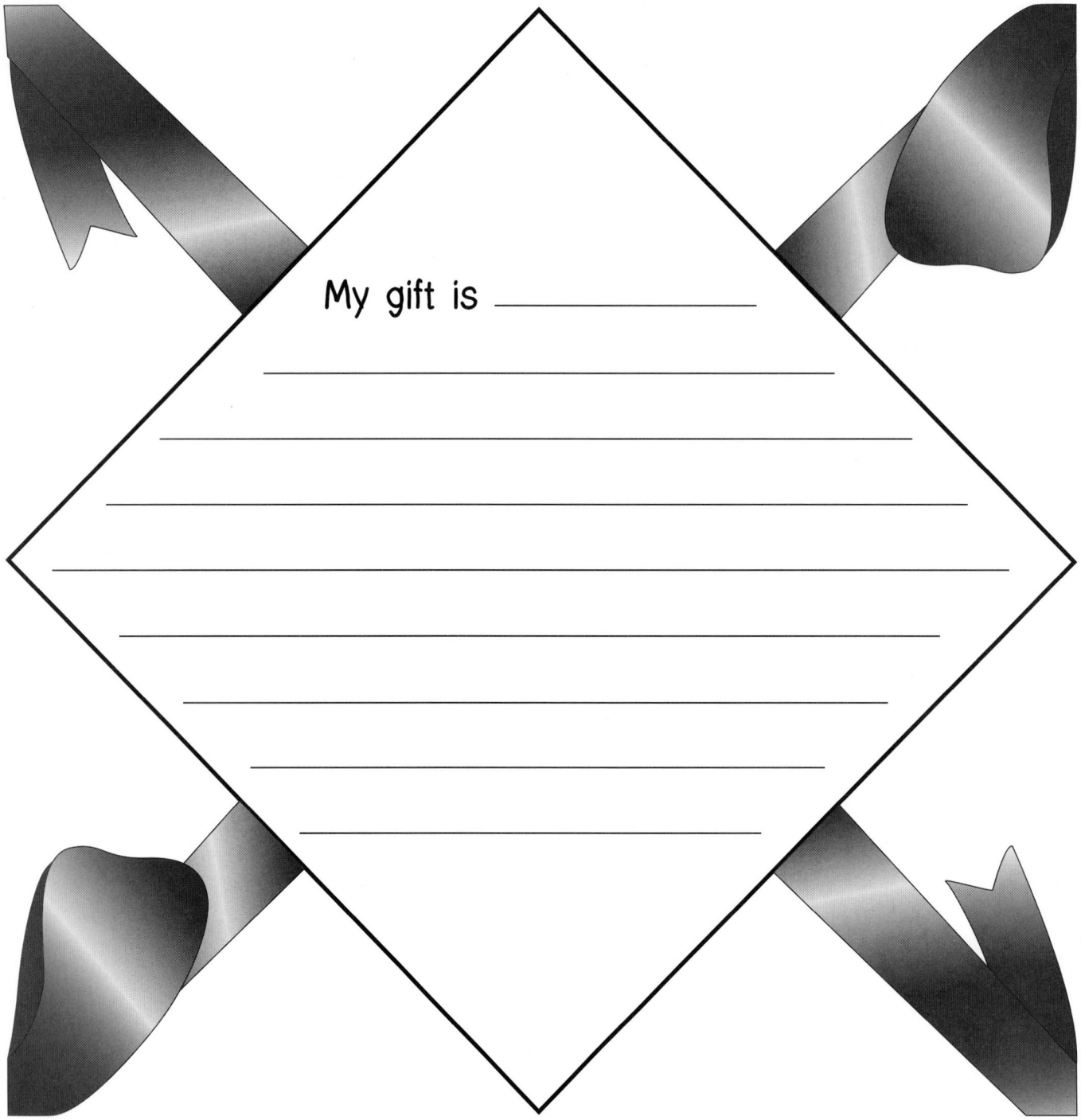

© Hampton-Brown

What Happens?

First,

Next,

Then,

Last,

© Hampton-Brown

My Sports Report

By _____

© Hampton-Brown

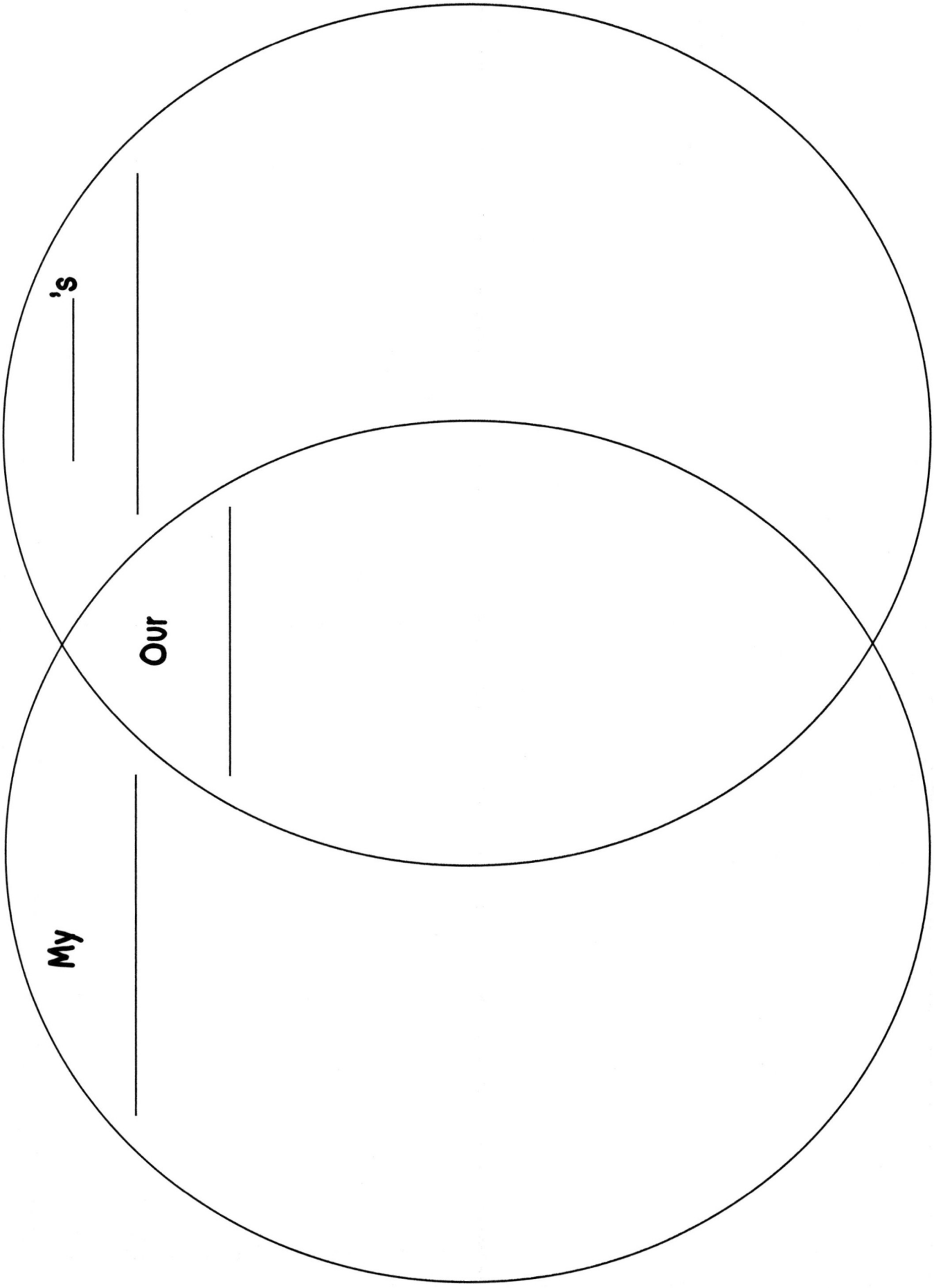

© Hampton-Brown

Our _____

© Hampton-Brown

Story Map

CHARACTERS

SETTING

PLOT

Beginning:

Middle:

End:

© Hampton-Brown

Title: _____

By _____

© Hampton-Brown

© Hampton-Brown

Main Idea: My favorite place is _____.

in front of | next to | behind | under | into

in back of | inside | across | over | on

My Favorite Place

By _____

© Hampton-Brown

A Story About Me

Main Idea:

Detail:

Detail:

Detail:

Detail:

© Hampton-Brown

Title: _____

By _____

_____

_____

_____

_____

_____

_____

_____

_____

_____

© Hampton-Brown

Dear Know-It-All,

My problem is: _____

_____

_____

_____

_____

_____

_____

My question is: _____

_____

_____

Thank you,

_____

© Hampton-Brown

Dear _____,

_____

_____

_____

_____

_____

_____

_____

_____

_____

_____

_____

_____

_____

Signed,

Know-It-All

© Hampton-Brown

What Happened

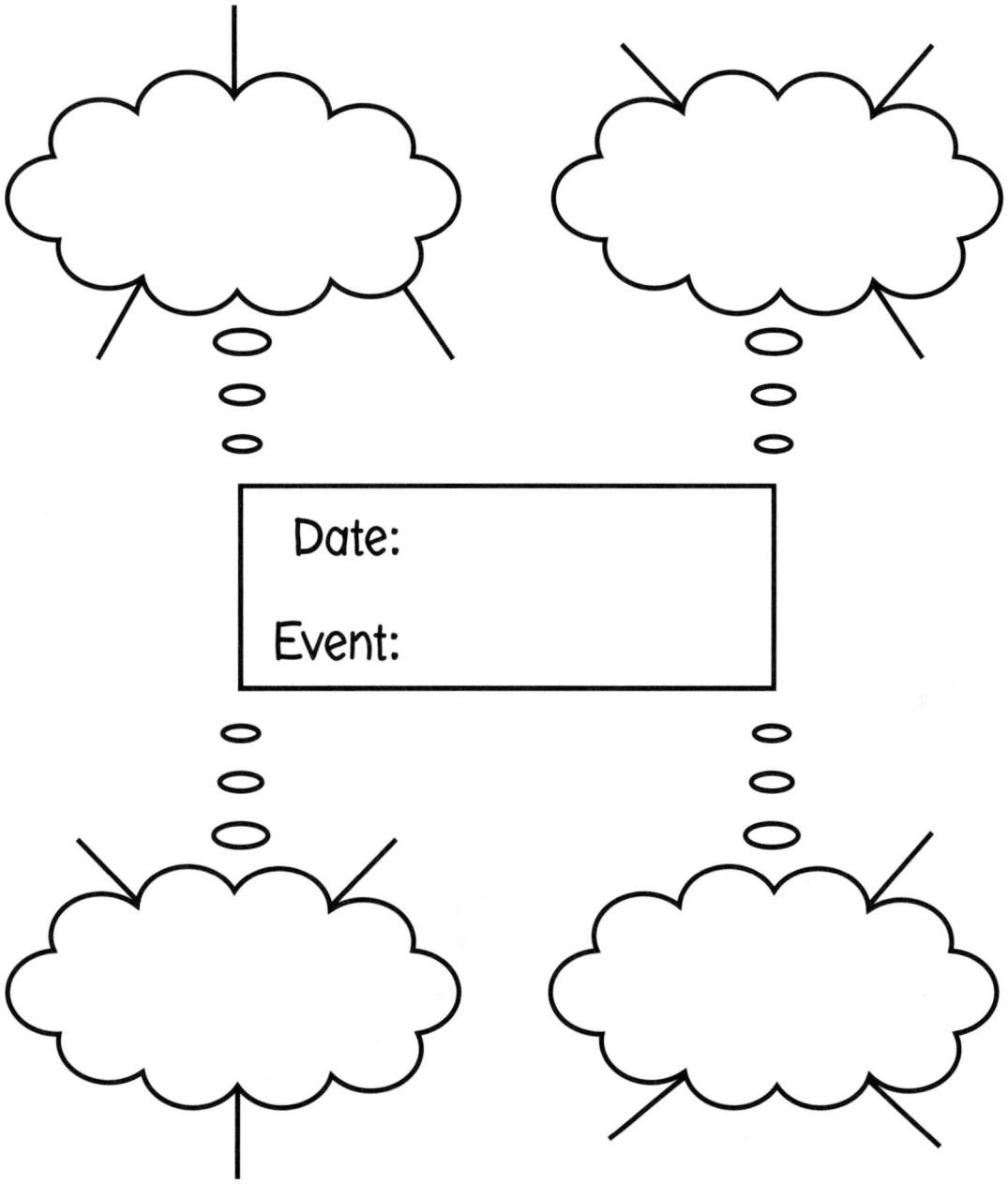

© Hampton-Brown

Date: _____

© Hampton-Brown

Our Script Planner

Question Starters

Do How

Does Why

Questions	Answers
_____ asks:	_____ answers:
_____ asks:	_____ answers:
_____ asks:	_____ answers:
_____ asks:	_____ answers:

© Hampton-Brown

Our Script

Character	Dialogue

This book is _____ than other books. It is _____

_____

_____

_____

_____

_____

_____

_____

_____

You ❑ should ❑ should not read this book!

My Review of:

Title: _____

By: _____

Illustrated by: _____

© Hampton-Brown

This book is about _____

Good things about this book:

Bad things about this book:

© Hampton-Brown

Skill Tests

Name _____ Date _____

Skill Test 1

DIRECTIONS Look at each picture. What word or words are missing? Mark your answer.

1. Ⓐ is
Ⓑ am
Ⓒ are
Ⓓ I'm

2. Ⓕ I
Ⓖ am
Ⓗ You
Ⓙ You're

3. Ⓐ is
Ⓑ am
Ⓒ are
Ⓓ I'm

4. Ⓕ The boots is
Ⓖ The boot are
Ⓗ The boots am
Ⓙ The boots are

© Hampton-Brown

Name _____ Date _____

Skill Test 2

DIRECTIONS Look at each picture. What word is missing? Mark your answer.

1. Ⓐ I
Ⓑ He
Ⓒ We
Ⓓ You

2. Ⓕ I
Ⓖ It
Ⓗ He
Ⓙ She

3. Ⓐ It
Ⓑ We
Ⓒ She
Ⓓ They

4. Ⓕ It
Ⓖ You
Ⓗ She
Ⓙ They

© Hampton-Brown

Name _____ Date _____

Skill Test 3

DIRECTIONS Look at each picture. What word or words are missing? Mark your answer.

1. Ⓐ I can
Ⓑ I, yes
Ⓒ Can you
Ⓓ Yes, you

2. Ⓕ Soup is it
Ⓖ Soup it are
Ⓗ Is the soup
Ⓙ Are the soup

3. Ⓐ Is the ball
Ⓑ The ball is
Ⓒ Where ball is
Ⓓ The ball where

4. Ⓕ Who
Ⓖ What
Ⓗ When
Ⓙ Where

© Hampton-Brown

Name _____ Date _____

Skill Test 4

DIRECTIONS Look at each picture. What words are missing? Mark your answer.

1. Ⓐ Is this
Ⓑ Can you
Ⓒ Open you
Ⓓ Please open

2. Ⓕ Can I
Ⓖ I have
Ⓗ Have I
Ⓙ What is

3. Ⓐ Is not
Ⓑ See you
Ⓒ Where is
Ⓓ Is where

4. Ⓕ not quiet are
Ⓖ are quiet not
Ⓗ not are quiet
Ⓙ are not quiet

© Hampton-Brown

Name _____ Date _____

Skill Test 5

DIRECTIONS Look at each picture. What words are missing? Mark your answer.

1. Ⓐ is eats
Ⓑ are eat
Ⓒ is eating
Ⓓ are eating

2. Ⓕ is plays
Ⓖ are play
Ⓗ is playing
Ⓙ are playing

3. Ⓐ Is he
Ⓑ Am he
Ⓒ He are
Ⓓ Are he

4. Ⓕ buying not am
Ⓖ not am buying
Ⓗ buying am not
Ⓙ am not buying

© Hampton-Brown

Name _____ Date _____

Skill Test 6

DIRECTIONS Look at each picture. What word or words are missing? Mark your answer.

1. Ⓐ a ducks
Ⓑ an ducks
Ⓒ three duck
Ⓓ three ducks

2. Ⓕ a orange
Ⓖ an orange
Ⓗ two orange
Ⓙ two oranges

3. Ⓐ mice
Ⓑ mices
Ⓒ mouse
Ⓓ mouses

4. Ⓕ child
Ⓖ childs
Ⓗ children
Ⓙ childrens

© Hampton-Brown

Name _____ Date _____

Skill Test 7

DIRECTIONS Look at each picture. What word or words are missing? Mark your answer.

1. Ⓐ that
Ⓑ two
Ⓒ three
Ⓓ square

2. Ⓕ big gift
Ⓖ gift big
Ⓗ little gift
Ⓙ gift little

3. Ⓐ grape is sweet
Ⓑ are grapes sweet
Ⓒ sweet grapes are
Ⓓ grapes are sweet

4. Ⓕ This
Ⓖ That
Ⓗ These
Ⓙ Those

© Hampton-Brown

Name _____ Date _____

Skill Test 8

DIRECTIONS Look at each picture. What words are missing? Mark your answer.

1. Ⓐ I jump
Ⓑ I jumps
Ⓒ They jump
Ⓓ They jumps

2. Ⓕ Play we
Ⓖ We play
Ⓗ We plays
Ⓙ Playing we

3. Ⓐ Monica climb
Ⓑ Monica climbs
Ⓒ Climbs Monica
Ⓓ Monica climbing

4. Ⓕ She has
Ⓖ Has she
Ⓗ She have
Ⓙ She haves

© Hampton-Brown

Name _____ Date _____

Skill Test 9

DIRECTIONS Look at each picture. What word is missing? Mark your answer.

1. Ⓐ Dad
Ⓑ Dads
Ⓒ Dads'
Ⓓ Dad's

2. Ⓕ I
Ⓖ my
Ⓗ his
Ⓙ their

3. Ⓐ Its
Ⓑ His
Ⓒ Her
Ⓓ Their

4. Ⓕ it
Ⓖ its
Ⓗ they
Ⓙ their

© Hampton-Brown

Name _____ Date _____

Skill Test 10

DIRECTIONS Look at each picture. What word is missing? Mark your answer.

1. Ⓐ like
Ⓑ likd
Ⓒ likes
Ⓓ liking

2. Ⓕ land
Ⓖ laned
Ⓗ landed
Ⓙ landing

3. Ⓐ jump
Ⓑ jumped
Ⓒ jumping
Ⓓ jumpped

4. Ⓕ hops
Ⓖ hoped
Ⓗ hopped
Ⓙ hopping

© Hampton-Brown

Name _____ Date _____

Skill Test 11

DIRECTIONS Look at each picture. What word is missing? Mark your answer.

1. Ⓐ in
Ⓑ on
Ⓒ below
Ⓓ behind

2. Ⓕ on
Ⓖ beside
Ⓗ behind
Ⓙ between

3. Ⓐ in
Ⓑ on
Ⓒ over
Ⓓ under

4. Ⓕ up
Ⓖ into
Ⓗ down
Ⓙ through

© Hampton-Brown

Name _____ Date _____

Skill Test 12

DIRECTIONS Look at each picture. What word is missing? Mark your answer.

1. Ⓐ are
Ⓑ had
Ⓒ was
Ⓓ were

2. Ⓕ take
Ⓖ took
Ⓗ taked
Ⓙ tooked

3. Ⓐ has
Ⓑ had
Ⓒ have
Ⓓ haved

4. Ⓕ ate
Ⓖ eat
Ⓗ ated
Ⓙ eated

© Hampton-Brown

Name _____ Date _____

Skill Test 13

DIRECTIONS Look at each picture. What word or words are missing? Mark your answer.

1. Ⓐ am
Ⓑ are
Ⓒ will
Ⓓ going

2. Ⓕ is going to
Ⓖ am going to
Ⓗ will going to
Ⓙ can going to

3. Ⓐ must
Ⓑ going
Ⓒ could
Ⓓ should

4. Ⓕ are
Ⓖ must
Ⓗ going
Ⓙ would

© Hampton-Brown

Name _____ Date _____

Skill Test 14

DIRECTIONS Look at each picture. What word is missing? Mark your answer.

1. Ⓐ it
Ⓑ me
Ⓒ you
Ⓓ them

2. Ⓕ me
Ⓖ we
Ⓗ you
Ⓙ him

3. Ⓐ me
Ⓑ her
Ⓒ him
Ⓓ them

4. Ⓕ it
Ⓖ us
Ⓗ him
Ⓙ them

© Hampton-Brown

Name _____ Date _____

Skill Test 15

DIRECTIONS Look at each picture. What words are missing? Mark your answer.

1. Ⓐ I do
Ⓑ Do you
Ⓒ You does
Ⓓ Does you

2. Ⓕ The bug do
Ⓖ Do the bug
Ⓗ Bug the does
Ⓙ Does the bug

3. Ⓐ Do are they
Ⓑ Are why they
Ⓒ Why are they
Ⓓ Why how they

4. Ⓕ How is
Ⓖ How are
Ⓗ How many
Ⓙ How much

© Hampton-Brown

Name _____ Date _____

Skill Test 16

DIRECTIONS Look at each picture. What word or words are missing? Mark your answer.

1. Ⓐ nice
Ⓑ nicer
Ⓒ niceer
Ⓓ nicest

2. Ⓕ the hotter day
Ⓖ hotter day than
Ⓗ hottest the day
Ⓙ the hottest day

3. Ⓐ more exciting
Ⓑ most exciting
Ⓒ more excitinger
Ⓓ most excitingest

4. Ⓕ best
Ⓖ better
Ⓗ bestest
Ⓙ goodest

© Hampton-Brown

ACKNOWLEDGMENTS

Illustrations

Karen Stormer Brooks: p12 (kite), p36, pp40-44, p46, p48, p89, pp91-103; **Joe Cepeda:** p19; **Eva Vagreti Cockrille:** p15; **Lynne Cravath:** p3, p4, pp6-11, p13, pp16-18, pp20-21, p22 (boy), pp25-26, p29, p32, p35, pp37-39, p88, p90; **Ruth Flanigan:** p22 (birthday illustrations), p23; **Peter Grosshauser:** pp49-51; **Jennifer Hewitson:** p27; **Maurie Manning:** p34; **Deborah Melmon:** p14, p31, p33; **Cheryl Kirk Noll:** p5, p24, p45, p47; **Ana Ochoa:** p28, p30; **Wendy Rasmussen:** p12 (lunch, swing, bread), p59.

Copyright © Hampton-Brown

All rights reserved.

Teachers are authorized to reproduce the materials contained in this book in limited quantities and solely for use in their classrooms.

Other than as authorized above, no part of this book may be reproduced or transmitted in any form or by any means, electronic or mechanical, including photocopying, recording, or by an information storage and retrieval system, without permission in writing from the publisher.

Hampton-Brown
P.O. Box 223220
Carmel, California 93922
800-333-3510
www.hampton-brown.com

Printed in the United States of America

ISBN 0-7362-2498-X

07 08 09 10 11 12 13 14 10 9 8 7 6 5 4